ALL ABOARD, FLORIDA!

WRITTEN BY MAGGIE AND ROSALIND BUNN

ILLUSTRATED BY KELLER PYLE

PELICAN PUBLISHING

New Orleans

Copyright © 2024
By Maggie Bunn and Rosalind Bunn

Illustrations copyright © 2024
By Harrison Keller Pyle
All rights reserved

Peace Pie is a registered trademark of Peace Pie LLC, depicted with permission.

The word "Pelican" and the depiction of a pelican are trademarks of Arcadia Publishing Company Inc. and are registered in the U.S. Patent and Trademark Office.

Library of Congress Cataloging-in-Publication Data

Names: Bunn, Maggie, author. | Bunn, Rosalind, author. | Pyle, Keller, illustrator.
Title: All aboard, Florida! / written by Maggie Bunn and Rosalind Bunn ; illustrated by Keller Pyle.
Description: New Orleans : Pelican Publishing, 2024. | Series: All aboard series ; vol 4 | Audience: Ages 5-8 | Audience: Grades 2-3 | Summary: "A child rides the train through Florida's varied landscapes. From the Panhandle to Big Bend, Clearwater, the Everglades, the Keys, Kennedy Space Center, Orlando, and St. Augustine, the narrator experiences the marvels of Florida"—Provided by publisher.
Identifiers: LCCN 2023023516 | ISBN 9781455627646 (hardcover)
Subjects: CYAC: Travelers—Fiction. | Railroads—Fiction. | Florida—Fiction. | LCGFT: Picture books.
Classification: LCC PZ7.1.B8646 Af 2024 | DDC [E]—dc23
LC record available at https://lccn.loc.gov/2023023516

Printed in China
Published by Pelican Publishing
New Orleans, LA
www.pelicanpub.com

To our Florida family—Kelly, Bill, Pierce, and Mary Charles and to our dear friend, Chris Negron.
—M. B. and R. B.

To my niece Olivia Paige, who brightens every day with her laughter and joy!
—H. K. P.

I was so excited. I could not wait to ride the train around Florida—my home state.

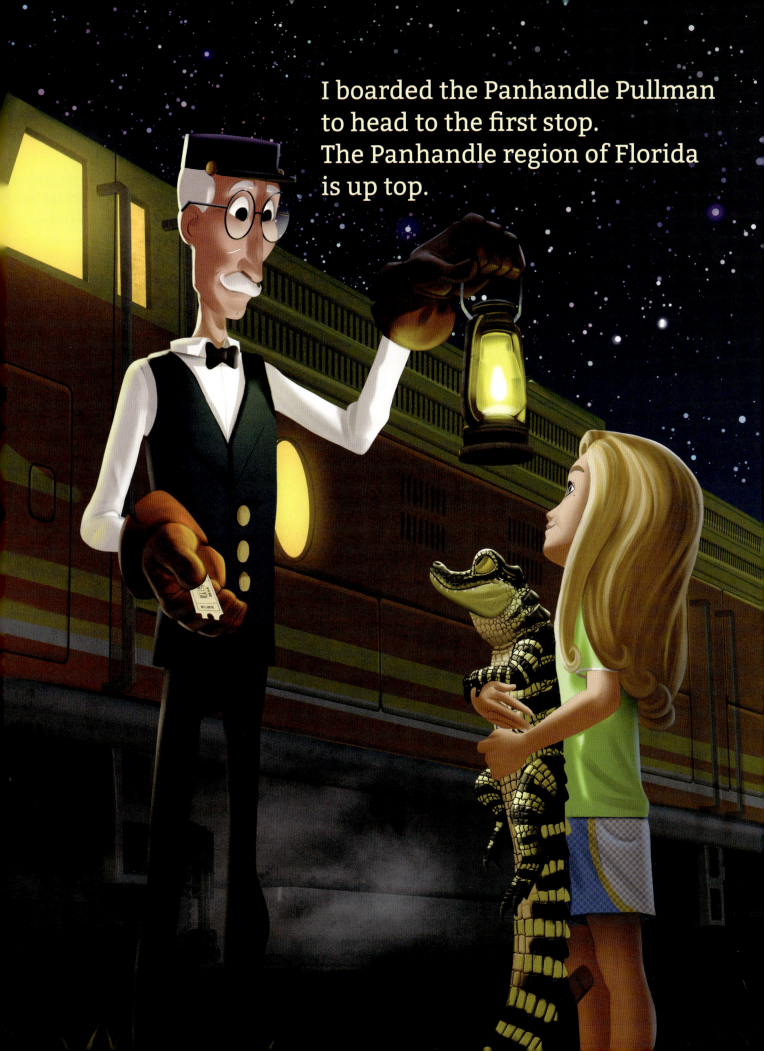

I boarded the Panhandle Pullman to head to the first stop. The Panhandle region of Florida is up top.

The emerald waters stretched for miles as we rode along.

The Pullman slowed to hear the shorebirds' early-morning song.

We made it to St. George Island as the sun rose. Manatees floated peacefully with the ocean's ebbs and flows.

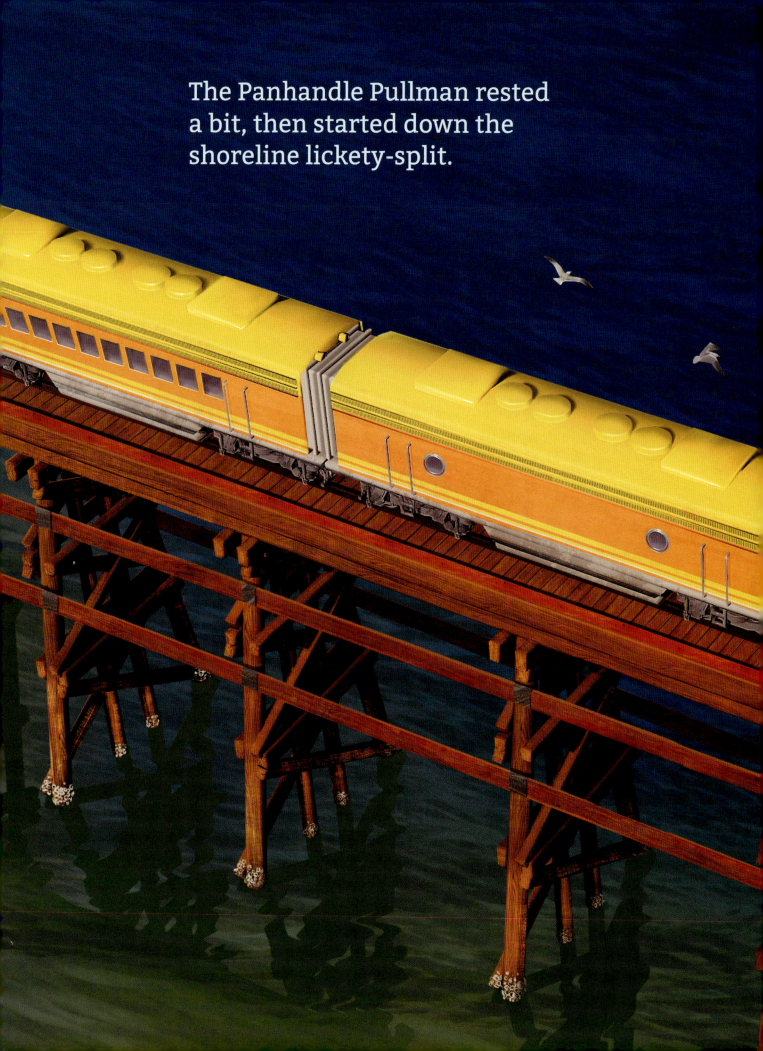
The Panhandle Pullman rested a bit, then started down the shoreline lickety-split.

We chugged to a halt at a new location. The Big Bend region of the Sunshine State was our next destination.

*We hopped on the Pullman.
We did not want to be late.
There's so much to see
around this great state!*

The West Florida Peninsula was the next region on the tracks. There just won't be much time to relax.

We saw so many sea turtles enjoying their stay. It won't be long until they are ready to be on their way.

We hopped on the Pullman.
We did not want to be late.
There's so much to see
around this great state!

GREEN SEA TURTLE

BOTTLENOSE DOLPHIN

We hopped on the Pullman.
We did not want to be late.
There's so much to
see around this
great state!

Across the Seven Mile Bridge, the Pullman made its way. Ernest Hemingway's house was next—so much to explore in one day.

The house stands frozen in time—where Papa penned his famous prose. You might even spot Snow White's descendants, each with extra toes.

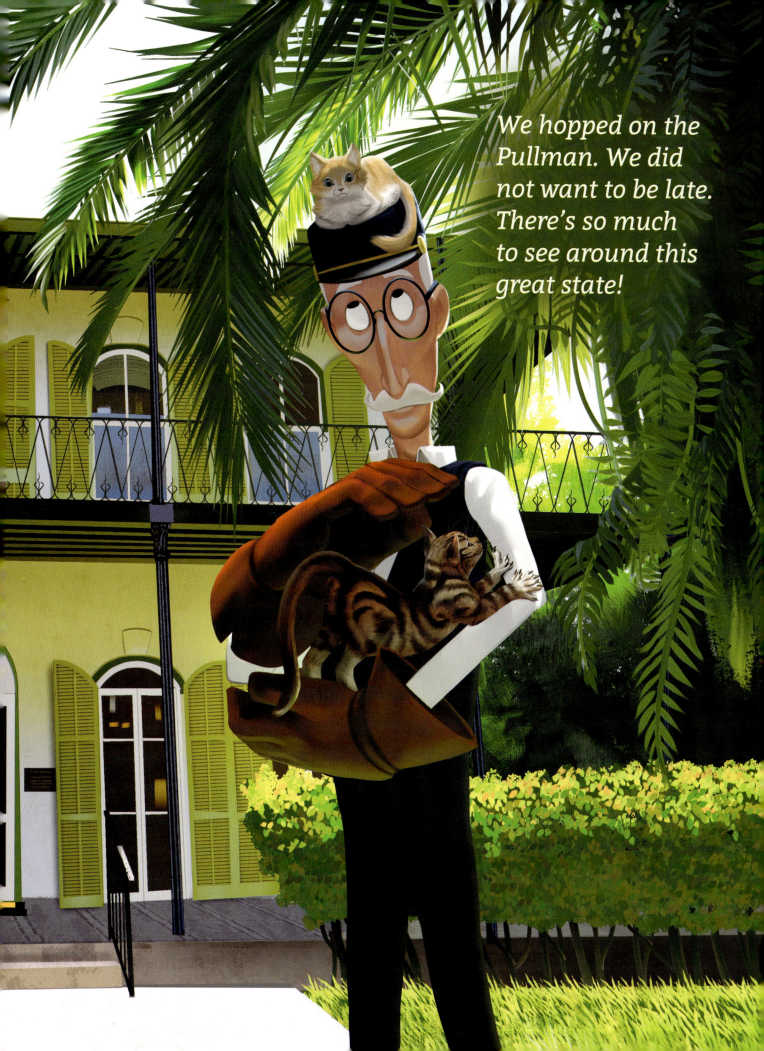

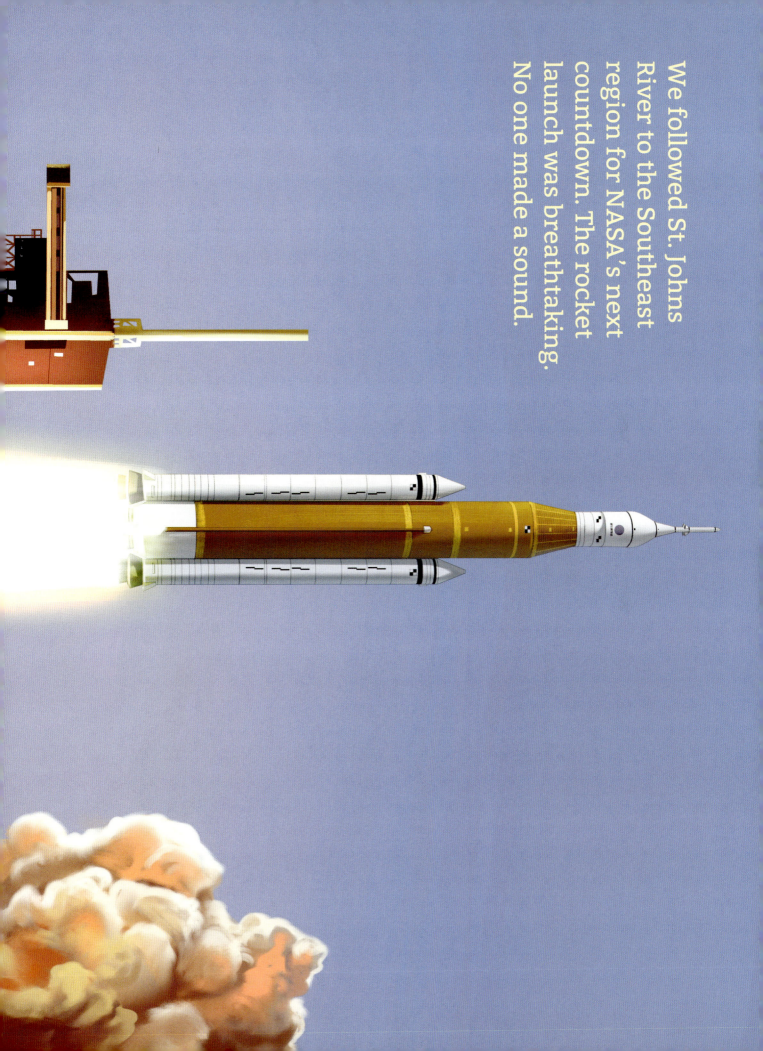

We followed St. Johns River to the Southeast region for NASA's next countdown. The rocket launch was breathtaking. No one made a sound.

We voted that a detour from our route had to be made. The carousel's lights flickered to its upbeat serenade.

We hopped on the Pullman. We did not want to be late. There's so much to see around this great state!

The Northeast region of the state was the last stop on the list. The Pullman slowed down so that nothing would be missed.

We feasted on Peace Pies
as we rode down Aviles Street.
St. Augustine, Florida's oldest city, was
beautiful, with so many tourists to meet.

Quenching our thirst
at the Fountain of
Youth, we took a
step back in history.
The magical powers
of Ponce de León's
find remains filled
with mystery.

There is buried treasure on Amelia Island, an old pirate legend tells. All we found were shark teeth and hundreds of seashells.

The sun was setting as we saw the lighthouse. The Pullman slowed down to let us climb out.

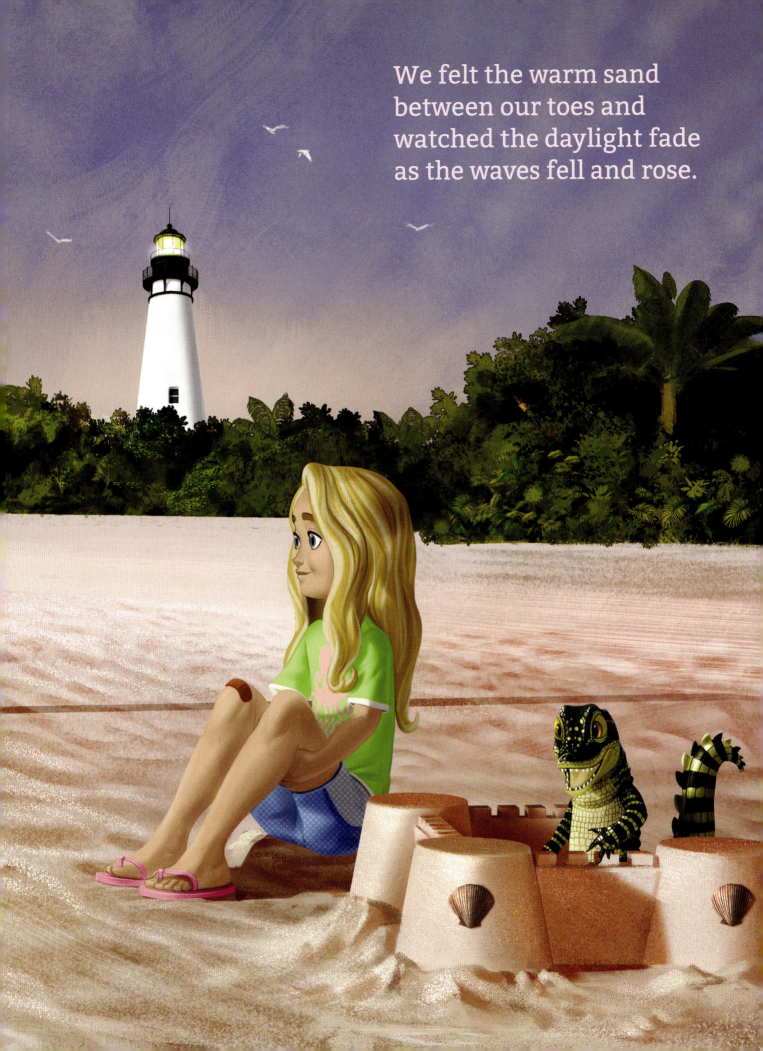

I grabbed my journal as the sun set to write about my adventures so I wouldn't forget.

My home state is amazing and here to explore. With so much to see, another trip is in store.
Choo, choo!

REGIONS OF FLORIDA

The Panhandle
The Panhandle of Florida is the narrow strip of land that is in Florida's northwest region. This area is known for its beautiful beaches, tourism, and resorts. Be careful, an occasional hurricane has been known to make an appearance.

Big Bend
This region is located along the western coast of Florida. Many wonderful animal species, including the Gulf sturgeon, West Indian manatee, piping plover, and red-cockaded woodpecker live in the marshland and woodlands located in this region. This area, abundant with natural resources, is considered the largest remaining undeveloped coastline in the contiguous United States.

West Florida Peninsula
This region is noted for its relatively high rainfall, averaging sixty-five inches annually. The state's largest port, Port Tampa Bay, is located here. The cities of St. Petersburg, Clearwater, and Tampa form one of Florida's largest metropolitan areas.

The Keys
The Florida Keys are a group of small islands located at the southern tip of Florida. Many of the keys fall within the boundaries of three national parks. Biscayne National Park includes several of the northernmost keys, while most of the keys in Florida Bay are within Everglades National Park and Dry Tortugas National Park, which includes historic Fort Jefferson. The western end is Key West (watch out for the roosters) with the Overseas Highway connecting all the main islands. The smaller islands of the Florida Keys are made from an ancient coral reef.

Southeast Florida
Florida's southeast region is sometimes called Treasure Coast. You never know when a pirate's lost gold will wash up on the beaches for you to find. This area is known for its beautiful, historic beaches and towns. St. Johns River flows from this region into Northeast Florida.

Northeast Florida
The Northeast region is also known as the "first coast." St. Augustine, the nation's oldest continuously settled city is in this region. It was founded in 1565, fifty-five years before the Pilgrims landed in Plymouth Rock. Amelia Island boasts many natural bird watching sites with thirteen miles of uncrowded beaches. In Fernandina Beach, the Visitor's Center is an old train depot that marked the northern terminus of Florida's first cross-state railway.